GET WRITING!

Charlotte Guillain

Raintree
Chicago, Illinois

© 2014 Raintree
an imprint of Capstone Global Library, LLC
Chicago, Illinois

To contact Capstone Global Library please phone 800-747-4992, or visit
our web site www.capstonepub.com

Edited by Rebecca Rissman, Dan Nunn, and Helen Cox Cannons
Designed by Steve Mead
Original illustrations © Capstone Global Library, Ltd
Picture research by Ruth Blair
Production by Vicki Fitzgerald
Originated by Capstone Global Library, Ltd
Printed and bound in China by CTPS

18 17 16
10 9 8 7 6 5 4 3 2

Library of Congress Cataloging-in-Publication Data
Guillain, Charlotte.
  Get Writing! / Charlotte Guillain.
     pages cm.—(Dream It, Do it!)
Includes bibliographical references and index.
ISBN 978-1-4109-6263-8 (hb)—ISBN 978-1-4109-6268-3 (pb) 1. Authorship.
2. Creative writing. 3. Authorship—Vocational guidance. I. Title.

PN145.G7786 2014
808.02—dc23   2013017423

Acknowledgments
The author and publisher are grateful to the following for permission to
reproduce copyright material: Capstone Publishers pp. 14 (Steve Mead),
26, 27, 28, 29 (all © Karon Dubke); Corbis p. 7 (© Ocean); Getty Images
pp. 11 (Jupiterimages); Raintree Publishers pp. 16 & 17 (Dawn Beacon);
Shutterstock pp. 4, 5 (© Jacek Chabraszewski), 7 (© Maxisport), 8 (©
vovan), 9 (© lineartestpilot), 10 (© 56836816), 12 left (© MisterElements),
12 right (© Ohmega1982), 13 left (© RetroClipArt), 13 right (© tsaplia),
15 (© ayelet-keshet), 19 (© Netfalls - Remy Musser), 20 (© Joana Kruse),
21 (© Linda Bucklin), 22 (© Lisa F. Young), 23 (© vovan), 24 (© Jacek
Chabraszewski), 25 (© AVAVA). Incidental photographs reproduced with
permission of Shutterstock.

Cover photograph of a young boy writing reproduced with permission
of Getty Images (kristian sekulic).

We would like to thank Adam Guillain for his invaluable help in the
preparation of this book.

CONTENTS

Be a Writer! 4

What to Write? 6

Collecting Ideas 8

Brainstorming! 10

Get to Know Your Characters 12

Draw Your Characters 14

Planning Your Story 16

Opening Lines 18

Set the Scene 20

Writing and Editing 22

Final Checks! 24

Make a Book 26

Glossary 30

Find Out More 31

Index 32

Some words are shown in bold, **like this**. You can find out what they mean by looking in the glossary.

BE A WRITER!

Have you always dreamed of being a writer? Would you love to write stories and share them with other people? This book will help you make your dreams come true.

Read on and find out how to stop dreaming and get writing!

WHAT TO WRITE?

Before you start, think about the type of story you'd like to write.

Do you want it to be:
- a funny story?
- an adventure story?
- a mystery story?
- a scary story?
- about friends or family?
- about school?

Or will your story be about something else?

Is your story for:
- children your age or younger than you?
- girls? boys? boys and girls?
- your friends?
- people you don't know?

Keep your reader in your head and talk to them as you write your story!

Your story

Will you write about:
- something that has happened to you?
- something you know a lot about, such as football, ponies, dancing, computer games, or something else?

Do you need to do any research before you start writing?

Will you write your story:
- set in the past, using **past tense**?
- as if it is happening now, in **present tense**?
- as if you are telling the story, in **first person**?
- as if someone else is telling the story, in **third person**?
- in a chatty voice or in a more formal way?

Look at some books you have enjoyed reading. What is the writer's voice like?

COLLECTING IDEAS

Lots of writers carry a notebook to collect ideas for stories. Make sure that you always have a pen and paper with you in case you have a great idea and want to remember it!

Girl hears a noise outside, looks out of window. Spaceship!

Inspiration

In your writer's notebook, draw an object, such as a chair, a car, a building—anything! Next, add features to the object as if you are turning it into an animal. What is it? Where does it come from? What does it want? Maybe this could be the start of a great story!

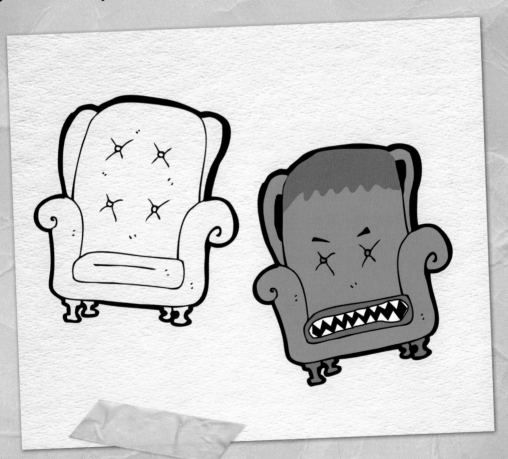

BRAINSTORMING!

Collect pictures that you like from magazines, the Internet, leaflets, or your own drawings. Stick them in your scrapbook or on a big piece of paper. Add pictures of people that you find in magazines, and think about who they could be. Make notes around the pictures.

Brainstorming with a friend can be double the fun!

GET TO KNOW YOUR CHARACTERS

The **characters** in your story are very important. You need to get to know them very well! Ask yourself questions about your characters.

Where are they from?

Do they have a family or any pets?

What do they want?

What clothes do they wear?

What three words could you use to describe each character?

How do they talk?

DRAW YOUR CHARACTERS

A good way to really get to know your **characters** is to draw pictures of them. Think about where to put their eyes and mouths.

Can you make them look happy, or sad, or angry?

Keep experimenting and ask yourself questions:

Who is this person?

What are they like?

Do they have any secrets?

PLANNING YOUR STORY

It is a good idea to plan your story before you start writing. Draw a story plan like the one shown here to show the main events in your story.

Pandarella's stepmother makes her work all day.

The prince invites everyone to the palace for a ball, but Pandarella's stepsisters say she can't go.

Pandarella's fairy godmother appears. "You shall go to the ball!"

Pandarella and the prince dance all evening. She must be home before midnight.

The clock strikes midnight. Pandarella runs home but loses a glass slipper on the way.

The prince searches for the owner of the slipper. He finds Pandarella. The slipper fits.

They live happily ever after!

Lots of good stories have a problem. Does your story have one? How is it solved? If you can, add a twist, or surprise event, at the end of your story.

OPENING LINES

All the best stories have a great opening that makes people want to read more. You could start with something funny, or perhaps start in the middle of the action. Try not to describe or explain things too much. This will keep your reader guessing.

Can you think of a story with a good opening? How and why does it make you want to read more?

SET THE SCENE

Once you have your story started, you will need to set the scene. This tells the reader all about the place where your story happens. Use your knowledge of the **senses** to imagine how the place looks, sounds, smells, and feels.

What might your senses tell you about a place like this?

Inspiration

Describe a scene for a friend to draw. Think very carefully about the words that you use. What time of day is it? What is the weather like? How tall is the house? Does your friend's picture match what you had in your head?

WRITING AND EDITING

As you write your story, try not to worry about making mistakes. Just try to tell your story in an exciting way. When you have finished, read it through. Are there places where you could make your writing more interesting? Could you move or cut out any parts to make the story flow better? This is called **editing**.

Inspiration

Try not to use the same words all the time. Write down any great new words you hear in your notebook so you can use them in your writing later.

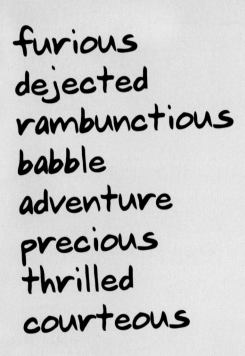

furious
dejected
rambunctious
babble
adventure
precious
thrilled
courteous

FINAL CHECKS!

When you are happy with the story you've written, check your spelling and **punctuation**! These are important to help your readers understand the story properly.

Activity

Read your story out loud to check how it sounds. Make a note if you stumble over any words, or if you have long sentences that could be **edited** to make them clearer.

MAKE A BOOK

Now make your story into a book!

1. Use a computer to type and print your story, or write it out neatly by hand. Leave spaces for **illustrations** if you want to include them.

2. If your story has chapters, make sure you have chapter headings. Draw any illustrations you want to put in your story.

3. Get a large piece of poster board to make a cover for your book. Ask an adult to help you staple the cover and pages in place.

4. Draw a picture on the front cover of your book. Make sure the title of your book and your name are clear.

5. On the back cover, write a blurb about your story. A blurb is a short description of your story that tells the reader what your book is about and makes them want to read it. Don't give too much away, though!

6. Have a book launch! Invite your friends and family, and have a party to celebrate your book. Make sure you have drinks and snacks for everyone! You could read a passage from your book and see if people have any questions about your story and how you wrote it.

7. Start thinking of ideas for your next story!

GLOSSARY

character person in a story, film, play, or television show

edit make changes to your writing, such as cutting or rewriting words, to improve it

experimenting thinking of different ideas and ways to do things

first person when a story is told from the point of view of one of the characters. First person uses "I" or "we."

illustration picture that shows a scene in a story

past tense describing events and actions that happened in the past

present tense describing events and actions that are happening now

punctuation marks, such as commas or question marks, that help show the meaning of a sentence

senses the fives senses are smelling, seeing, hearing, tasting, and touching

third person when a story is told by someone who is not involved in the story. Third person uses "he," "she," or "they."

FIND OUT MORE

Books

Fandel, Jennifer and Jan Fields. *You Can Write* (series). Mankato, Minn: Capstone, 2013.

Loewen, Nancy. *Writer's Toolbox* (series). Mankato, Minn.: Picture Window, 2011.

Web sites

FactHound offers a safe, fun way to find Internet sites related to this book. All of the sites on FactHound have been researched by our staff.

Here's all you do:

Visit www.facthound.com

Type in this code: 9781410962638

INDEX

book launch 28
book, making a
  26–29
brainstorming 10
chapters 26
characters 12–15,
  30
description 18
editing 22, 25
first and third person
  6, 30
ideas 8–9
illustrations 26, 30
new words 23
notebooks 8, 23

openings 18
past and present
  tense 6, 30
planning your story
  16–17
problems and twists
  17
reading out loud
  25, 28
research 6
scene, setting the
  20–21
spelling and
  punctuation 24, 30
stories, types of 6
story maps 16–17